Health Facts

All About Your

Heart and Blood

Donna Bailey

STECK-VAUGHN
LIBRARY
A Division of Steck-Vaughn Company

Austin, Texas

How to Use This Book

This book tells you many things about your heart and blood. There is a Table of Contents on the next page. It shows you what each double page of the book is about. For example, pages 12 and 13 tell you about "How the Heart Works."

On most of these pages you will find some words that are printed in **bold** type. The bold type shows you that these words are in the Glossary on pages 46 and 47. The Glossary explains the meaning of words that may be new to you.

At the very end of the book there is an Index. The Index tells you where to find certain words in the book. For example, you can use it to look up words like arteries, blood pressure, ventricle, and many other words to do with your heart and blood.

Printed and bound in the United States
1 2 3 4 5 6 7 8 9 0 LB 95 94 93 92 91

Library of Congress Cataloging-in-Publication Data

Bailey, Donna.
  All about your heart and blood / Donna Bailey.
    p. cm.—(Health facts)
  Rev. ed. of: The heart and blood / Jan Burgess. 1988.
  Includes index.
  Summary: Discusses how the heart and circulatory system work, the functions of blood, how doctors help people with blood and heart disorders, and how to keep the cardiovascular system healthy through diet and exercise.
  ISBN 0-8114-2779-X
  1. Cardiovascular system—Juvenile literature.
2. Blood—Juvenile literature. 3. Heart—Juvenile literature. [1. Circulatory system. 2. Blood.
3. Heart.] I. Burgess, Janet, 1952– Heart and blood. II. Title. III. Series: Bailey, Donna. Health facts.
QP103.B35 1990   90-10052
612.1—dc20   CIPAC

Contents

Introduction   4   Body Controls   28
The First Doctors   6   Healing   30
Finding Out   8   Blood Types   32
Around the Body   10   New Blood for Old   34
How the Heart Works   12   Illnesses   36
Blood Vessels   14   Making People Better   38
Your Heartbeat   16   First Aid   40
Blood and the Lungs   18   Health and Your Heart   42
What Is Blood Made Of?   20   Staying Healthy   44
Fighting Disease   22
Fuel and Waste   24   Glossary   46
A Warm Body   26   Index   48

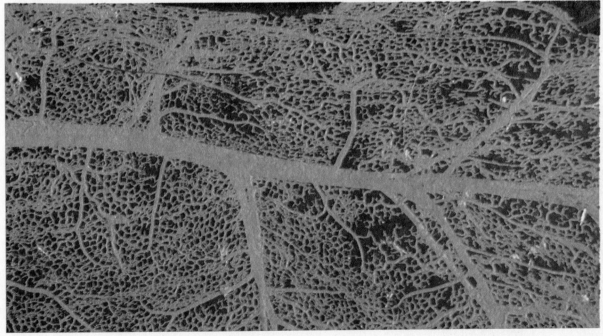

Introduction

When you have been running and are out of breath, you can feel your heart beating on the left-hand side of your chest.

Your heart started beating before you were born, when you were still inside your mother. Your heart pumps a red liquid called blood to every part of your body. Blood helps babies to grow when they are still inside their mother.

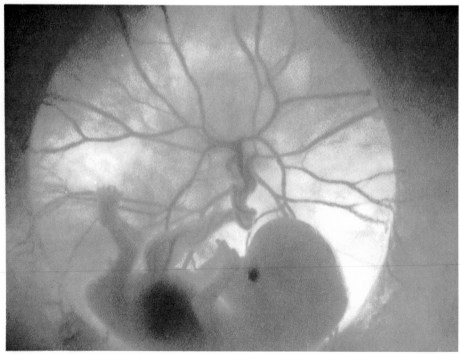

blood keeps us alive before we are born

Your heart beats all the time and keeps you alive. A child's heart beats at 80 to 100 times a minute. An adult's heart beats at 60 to 80 times a minute. The heart works with the other parts of the body.

your heart pumps blood to every part of your body

when birds fly, they need a lot of blood pumped to their bones, so their hearts beat very fast and are quite big

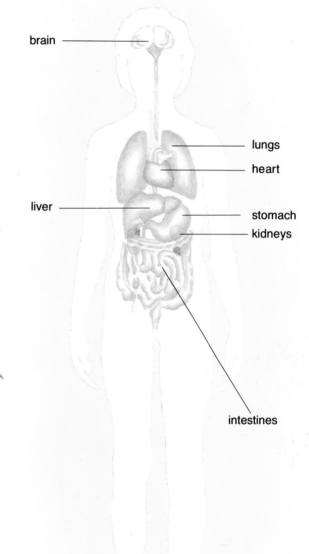

brain

lungs

heart

liver

stomach

kidneys

intestines

heart

ribs

The First Doctors

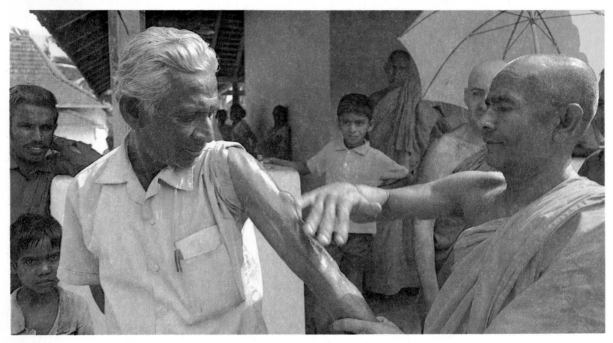

The picture shows a monk in India treating a man with a snake bite. This way of curing snake bites has been used for thousands of years. The first doctors used plants, herbs, and animals like mice and frogs to make medicines.

Today, scientists know how the body works. They have found cures for many different illnesses. They are always looking for more cures.

people have
been saying
prayers to
cure the
sick for a
long time

The first doctors knew that the heart
and blood were important, but they
did not know how the body worked.
They thought that disease was
caused by bad magic, or by devils and
spirits. People said prayers over
patients and sick people visited holy
places to pray for cures.

Finding Out

William Harvey talking to King Charles I

People thought if you made a patient bleed, they would get better. Doctors kept water creatures called leeches for **blood-letting.**

In 1628 William Harvey, an Englishman, was the first person to explain how blood travels around the body.

a leech used for blood-letting

Anton van Leeuwenhoek was one of the first people to use a **microscope.** He made many microscopes. Some of them made things look 300 times larger. Doctors could now look at blood and see what it was made up of.

Leeuwenhoek saw that blood is made of tiny bits called blood **cells.**

We cannot see inside our bodies, but we can hear what is going on. René Laënnec was the first person to listen to a patient's heartbeat. He used a wooden tube called a **stethoscope.**

**the first microscopes
did not look like the
ones doctors use today**

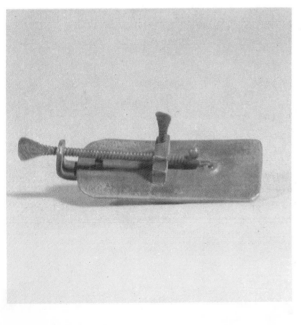

**Leeuwenhoek raised his
microscope to his eye to
look at things**

Around the Body

As you breathe, you take in a gas called **oxygen.** The oxygen goes down your **windpipe** into your **lungs.**

Your lungs are covered with tiny **blood vessels.** The blood flowing through the blood vessels picks up oxygen from your lungs and takes it to your heart. Your heart then pumps the blood around your body.

Oxygen-filled blood goes from your heart along your **arteries** into a network of tiny tubes, or **capillaries.** Capillaries pass oxygen from your blood into the cells that surround them.

Tiny blood vessels called **veins** take the stale blood with no oxygen in it back from the cells to your heart. Your heart then pumps this stale blood to your lungs to pick up more oxygen.

If you put the fingers of one hand on the inside of your other wrist, just above your thumb, you can count the beats of your heart. The number of beats you count per minute is your **pulse rate.**

taking someone's pulse

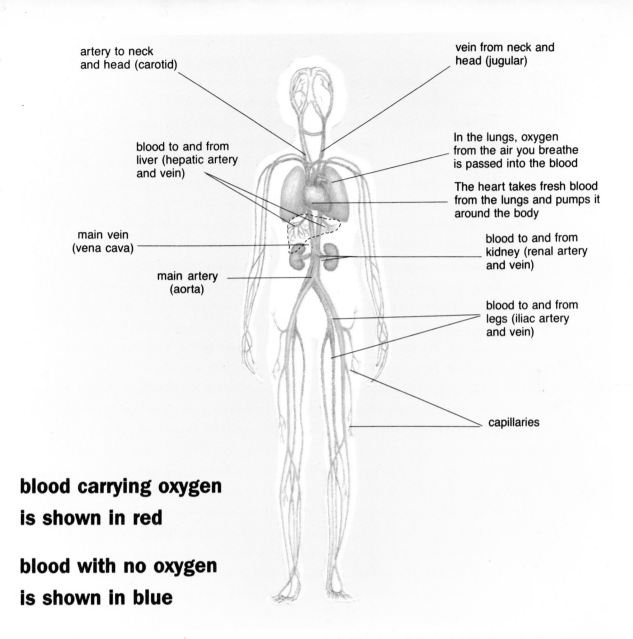

artery to neck
and head (carotid)

vein from neck and
head (jugular)

blood to and from
liver (hepatic artery
and vein)

In the lungs, oxygen
from the air you breathe
is passed into the blood

The heart takes fresh blood
from the lungs and pumps it
around the body

main vein
(vena cava)

blood to and from
kidney (renal artery
and vein)

main artery
(aorta)

blood to and from
legs (iliac artery
and vein)

capillaries

**blood carrying oxygen
is shown in red**

**blood with no oxygen
is shown in blue**

Did You Know?

☆ A normal heart beats about 2.5 billion times in an
average lifetime.

☆ There are about 60,000 miles of blood vessels in
a human body.

☆ A drop of blood goes around the body more than
1,000 times a day.

☆ It takes just one minute for a drop of blood to go
from your heart, down to your toes and all the way
back again.

☆ Blood leaves the heart traveling at three feet a
second.

☆ A baby has only about one quart of blood. A child
has about three quarts of blood. An adult has a
little more than five quarts of blood.

How the Heart Works

Your heart is a big, powerful **muscle.**
Inside your heart are four different
spaces called **chambers.**
Stale blood collects in the top right
chamber, called the right **atrium.**
From there, stale blood passes
through **valves** to the right **ventricle.**
The blood is then pushed out to the
lungs where it loads up with oxygen.

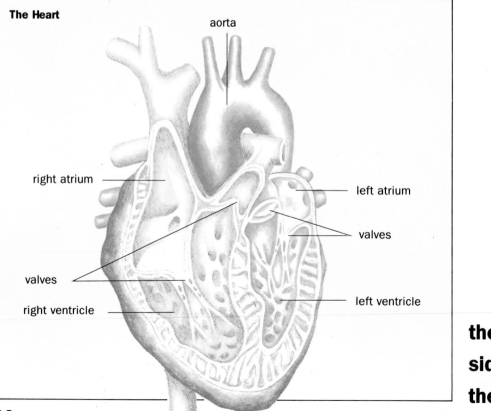

The Heart

aorta

right atrium

left atrium

valves

valves

left ventricle

right ventricle

**the two
sides of
the heart**

Blood from your lungs collects in the left atrium, then passes down into the left ventricle. There a strong muscle pumps blood around the body. Valves stop blood in the two sides of the heart from mixing together.

athletes' hearts beat faster after a race

how blood flows in and out of the heart

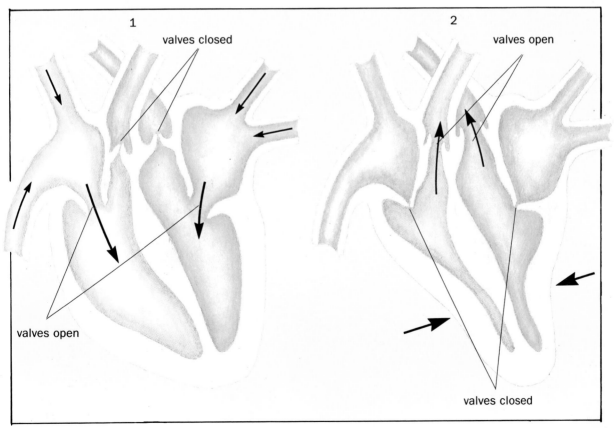

1

valves closed

valves open

2

valves open

valves closed

Blood Vessels

The picture shows the network of tiny capillaries that carry oxygen-filled blood to the **kidneys.** Blood vessels also carry **nutrients** to all the different cells in your body.

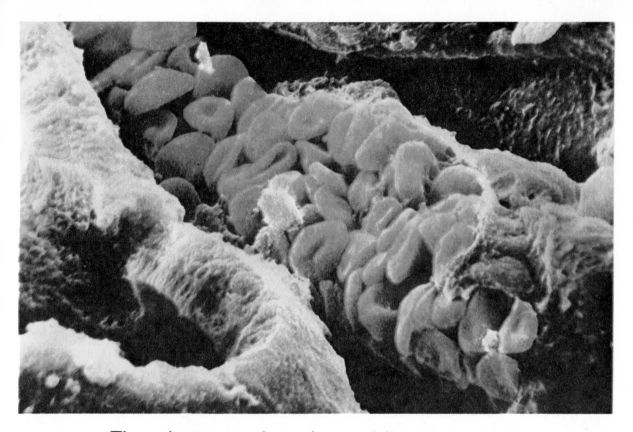

The photograph, taken with a powerful microscope, shows the cells in blood.

The heart squeezes blood out into the arteries with great force. The walls of the arteries have to be strong and elastic because the blood is under **pressure.** The walls of veins are not as strong because blood going back to the heart in veins is no longer under pressure. Tiny valves inside the veins prevent the blood from flowing backward.

Your Heartbeat

The push that your heart gives to your blood is called your blood pressure. Each time your heart beats, this wave of pressure makes a **pulse** that flows out along your arteries.

If you run or skip, you will notice that your pulse rate will be faster after the exercise than before it.

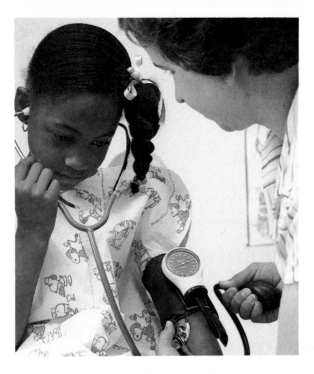

measuring blood pressure

A measurement of blood pressure is always in two numbers, for example $\frac{90}{60}$. The higher number is the pressure when the heart squeezes the blood and the lower one is the pressure between beats.

even if you stand upside down, your blood still flows around your body

When you exercise, the muscles you use need extra food and oxygen, so your heart pumps faster to send them extra blood.

A doctor can check your blood pressure by wrapping a band around your arm and pumping air into it. The doctor then measures the pressure of your blood on a **gauge.**

Blood and the Lungs

Your lungs are covered by your **ribs.**
When you breathe in, a muscle called
your **diaphragm** at the bottom of your
ribs flattens and pulls downward.
This makes the space in your lungs
larger and the air is pulled in.
When you breathe out, your rib
muscles and diaphragm relax, your
diaphragm moves upward and air is
pushed out.

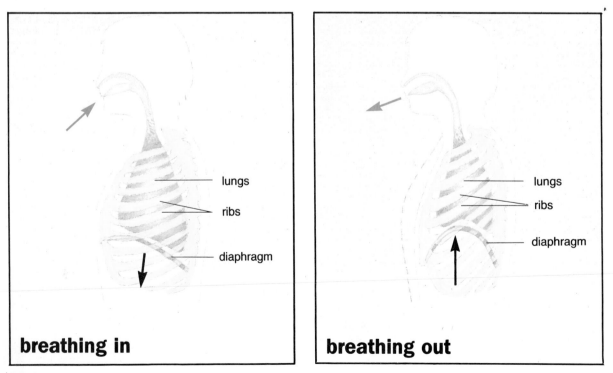

lungs

ribs

diaphragm

breathing in

lungs

ribs

diaphragm

breathing out

plants give out oxygen

Your lungs are like large sponges full of tiny holes called **alveoli.** Alveoli are covered with tiny capillaries that pass oxygen from the air into the bloodstream. **Carbon dioxide** passes back from the blood into your lungs and is breathed out.

air

capillary carrying carbon dioxide from bloodstream

capillary carrying oxygen into bloodstream

alveolus

lungs

What Is Blood Made Of?

The picture shows doctors looking at blood cells through microscopes. They can count the different kinds of cells and check their size and shape.

Blood is made up of different kinds of cells and each has its own job to do. Red blood cells carry oxygen and food. They collect the waste carbon dioxide in our bodies and take it to the lungs where we breathe it out.

white blood cells

There are two white blood cells for every 1,000 of the smaller red blood cells. White blood cells can change shape and fight the **germs** in your body which make you ill.

If you cut yourself, tiny blood cells called **platelets** stick together. They stop the bleeding and make a **scab** over the cut.

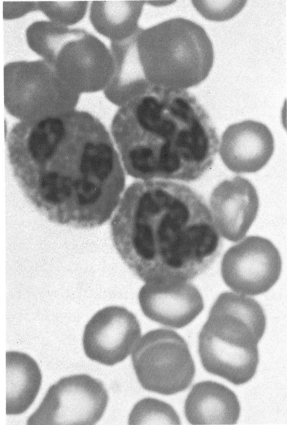

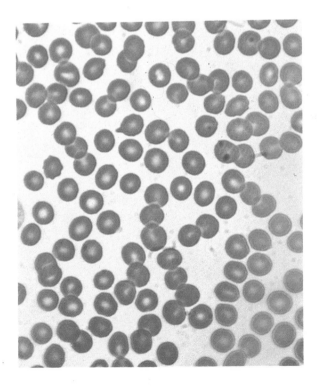

Capillaries are so small that red blood cells have to squeeze through them in single file.

red blood cells

Did You Know?

☆ Red blood cells are made at a rate of 90 to 100 million a minute.

☆ Red blood cells live for about 4 months.

☆ White blood cells live for about 7 to 14 days.

☆ Platelets live for about 8 to 10 days.

☆ One red blood cell makes 170,000 journeys around the body in its lifetime.

☆ In every drop of blood there are 250 million red blood cells, 100,000 white blood cells and 15 million platelets.

Fighting Disease

The small, round shape at the bottom left of the picture is a germ. A white blood cell surrounds the germ and swallows it. A white blood cell can also make an **antibody** to kill the germ.

Doctors can make you **immune** to some diseases by giving you a **vaccination.**

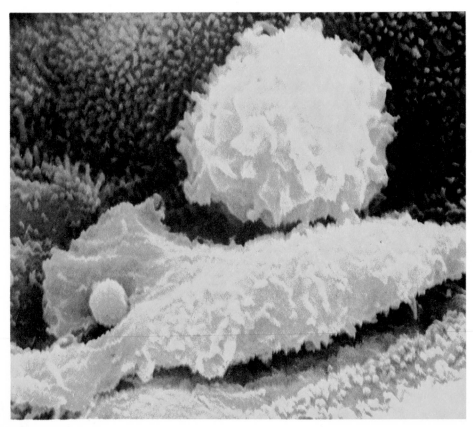

the lymphatic system

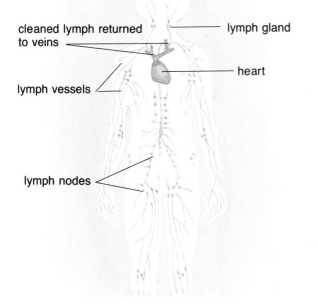

cleaned lymph returned to veins

lymph gland

heart

lymph vessels

lymph nodes

A clear liquid called **lymph** flows through the lymphatic system in our bodies. Lymph nodes along the system and in our **glands** hold extra white cells to help attack harmful germs.

giving a vaccination

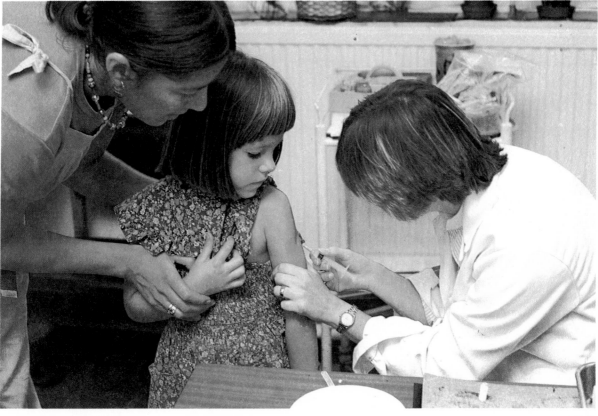

Fuel and Waste

Our bodies need food to give us **energy** to move. Your **digestive system** breaks down the food you eat into tiny pieces which can then pass into your blood.

When you swallow your food, muscles push it down your throat to your stomach, which churns and breaks up the food.

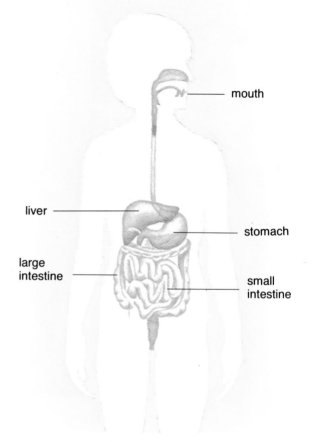

the digestive system

mouth

liver

stomach

large intestine

small intestine

inside the small intestine

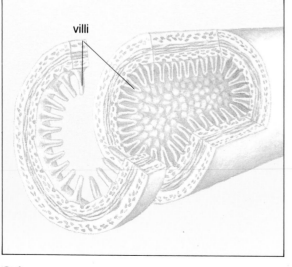

villi

The partly-digested food then moves into your small intestine, which finishes digesting food. The inside walls of the small intestine have thousands of tiny **villi** which pass the tiny bits of digested food into your blood.

24

The solid waste material left over when digestion is finished, now goes into the large intestine. Here extra water taken out of this waste is passed back into the blood.

Your blood flows through filters in your kidneys hundreds of times every day so that the water in the blood gets cleaned. Most of this water goes back into the bloodstream.

Urea, or waste water drains into your **bladder.** You empty your bladder and get rid of the solid waste left over from digestion when you go to the toilet.

kidneys clean the blood

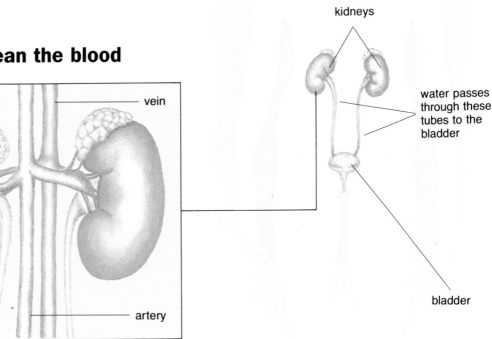

The Kidneys

vein

filters

artery

kidneys

water passes through these tubes to the bladder

bladder

A Warm Body

Some animals, like the lizard in the picture are cold-blooded. Their bodies can't make their own heat. They move very slowly when it's cold. They need the sun to keep them warm.

Human beings are warm-blooded. We make our own heat so our bodies stay at the same **temperature.**

the sun warms the lizard's body

When we eat food, our blood carries the heat we make to all parts of our bodies. When we exercise, our muscles give out heat. Blood vessels under the skin give off the extra heat through the skin and help to cool down the body.

taking a temperature

this girl is feeling hot

Normal body temperature is about 98.6°F. This goes up when you are ill because your body is fighting germs. We use a strip **thermometer** on the forehead to take the temperature of a young child. A glass thermometer is put under the tongue of an older person to take a temperature.

27

Body Controls

Each day our bodies follow a pattern of sleep, work, play, and eating meals. Our blood carries **hormones** which control our bodies and act as messengers to tell different parts of our bodies what to do.

Hormones made in one kind of gland pass into the bloodstream. Each gland makes a special hormone to do a certain job, such as controlling our heart rate, or telling our bodies how quickly to digest food, or how much water we need.

Hormones made in other glands act directly on one part of the body and do not go into the bloodstream.

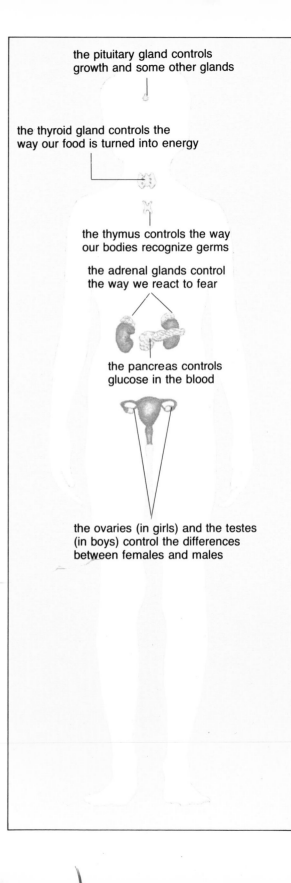

the pituitary gland controls growth and some other glands

the thyroid gland controls the way our food is turned into energy

the thymus controls the way our bodies recognize germs

the adrenal glands control the way we react to fear

the pancreas controls glucose in the blood

the ovaries (in girls) and the testes (in boys) control the differences between females and males

At the start of a race, the racing driver in our picture below feels nervous and excited. The hormone adrenalin is working in his body. It makes his heart beat faster so that more blood flows to his muscles. Adrenalin makes our bodies ready for action when we feel excited or scared.

measuring growth

The hormone made in our **pituitary gland** controls how much we grow. People without enough growth hormone do not grow as fast as they should. They will be shorter than normal. Too much growth hormone means a person will grow taller than normal.

Healing

When you cut yourself, dirt and germs can easily get into the wound. Platelets in your blood form a **clot** over the cut until the new skin can grow over the wound.

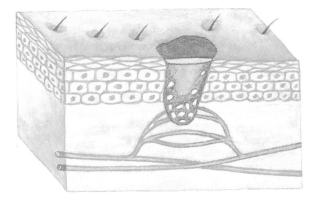

white blood cells kill the germs in the cut

platelets stick together and fibrin makes a scab

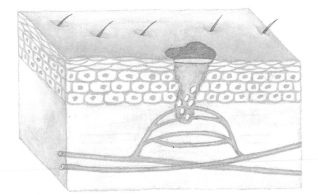

new skin starts to grow under the scab

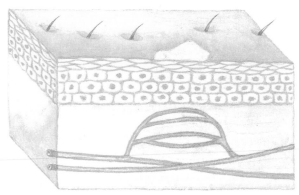

when the skin is healed, the scab falls off

30

The picture shows how a wound looks through a microscope. A network of thin strands of **fibrin** is trapping the blood cells. This makes the blood clot and seal the hole. A solid scab slowly builds up over the wound to prevent dirt and germs from getting into your body.

In the picture the red blood cells are shown in yellow so you can see them more easily.

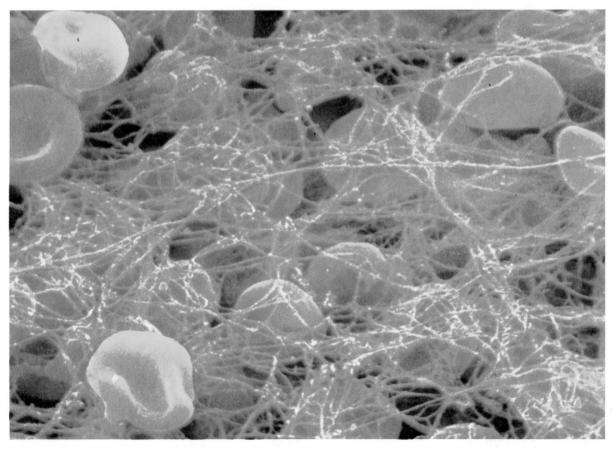

Blood Types

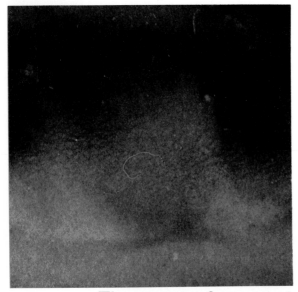 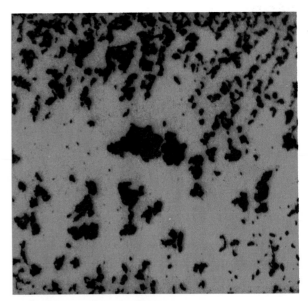

There are four main types or groups of blood, called A, B, AB, and O.

The photos, taken under a microscope, show (on the left) two blood groups that have mixed very well. On the right the two blood groups have not mixed well. The red cells have clumped together.

If blood from group A is given to someone with group B blood, the **antigens** in the B blood will try to kill the cells in the A blood and the person can get very sick.

People from the same part of the world often belong to the same blood group. Many South American Indians, like this family from Peru, are group O.

Blood must be carefully matched to make sure it will mix safely. If a patient loses a lot of blood after an accident, doctors must find out what blood group she or he is.

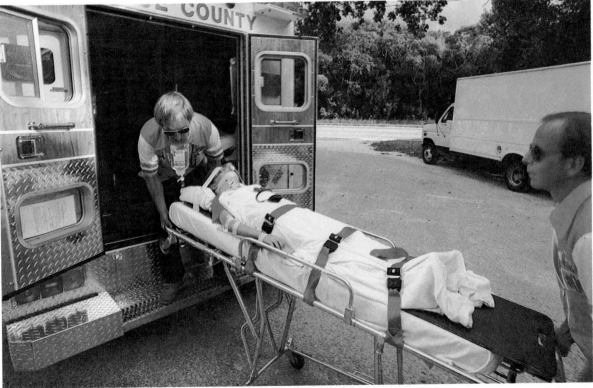

New Blood for Old

The picture shows blood being given to a patient during an operation.

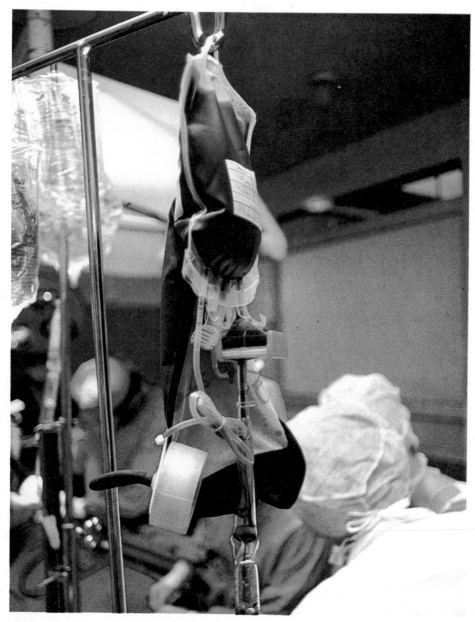

the blood is stored in the bag and given to the patient when needed

The blood is given by a **donor** with the same group. An adult donor can give about a pint of blood.

a blood bank

When a donor gives blood, a needle is put into a vein in their arm. The blood flows along a thin tube into a container. This has **chemicals** in it which keep the blood from clotting, and special food to keep the cells alive.

The donor's blood is then tested, labeled, and stored in a **blood bank** at 39°F to keep it fresh.

giving blood helps save lives and does not harm the donor

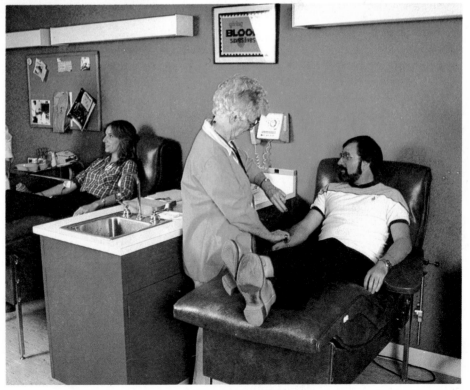

Illnesses

If a person eats too much fatty food, fatty **deposits** narrow the arteries.

When the arteries of our heart get blocked like the one in the picture, the blood supply is cut off.
This may cause a **heart attack** and the heart may stop beating.

Narrowed Arteries

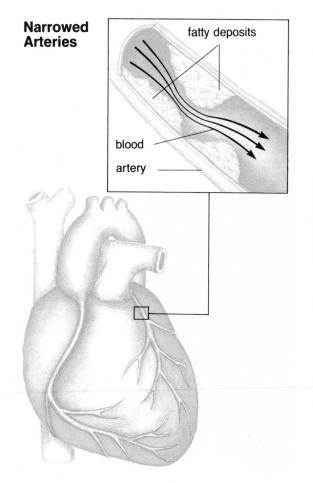

fatty deposits

blood

artery

Some people are born with blood that
does not clot properly, so even a
tiny cut is dangerous because it is
difficult to stop the bleeding.
This illness is called **hemophilia.**
Medical treatment helps people with
hemophilia to lead active lives, but
they must take care not to get cut.

Making People Better

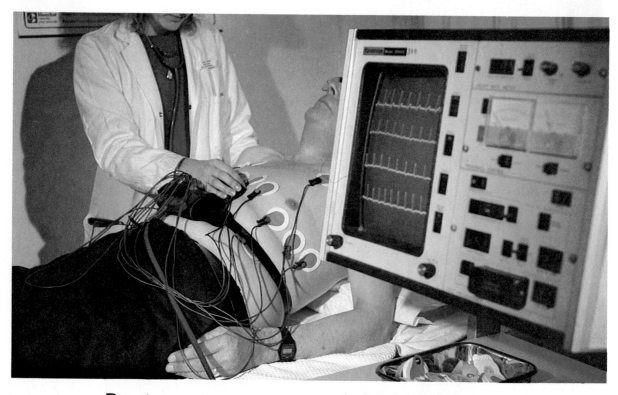

Doctors can use a special machine to
find out if a patient's heart is beating
properly. Special pads put on the
patient's body pick up electrical
signals from the heart which show up
as a pattern on the screen. Doctors
can decide from this pattern which
part of the heart is not working
properly. Doctors can then operate to
correct the problem.

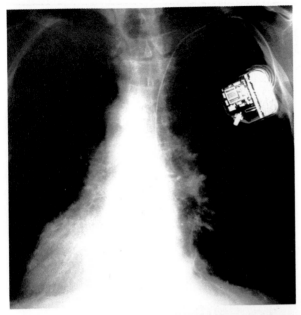

The **X-ray** photo shows the inside of a person's chest. A **pacemaker** is helping the person's heart to beat.

Samples of patients' blood which are tested under a microscope also help to find out if they are suffering from a disease.

testing samples of blood

First Aid

When there is an accident, you can sometimes help someone before a doctor or an ambulance arrives. You must stay calm and know exactly what to do. Groups like the Red Cross run courses to teach people first aid.

if someone has a heart attack, call an ambulance

if someone feels faint, make them sit with their head between their knees

if you have a nose blood, pinch your nose gently to stop the bleeding

40

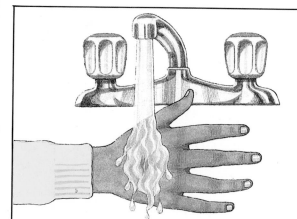

if you have a cut or a scratch,
wash it first under running
cold water, then dry the wound
and put a bandage on it

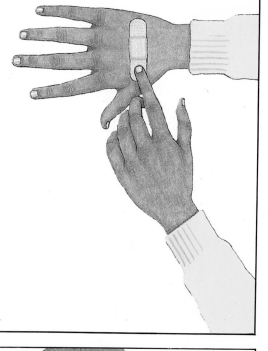

if blood is spurting out from
a cut, use a clean cloth to
press down hard on the wound
until you can get help

Health and Your Heart

People in the United States and Europe get more heart disease than people in Africa or Asia because they eat a lot of fatty foods. Fatty food can block up the arteries.

Your heart and blood need nutrients to keep healthy, such as the iron and vitamins found in vegetables.

When people fill their lungs with cigarette smoke, it covers their lungs with tar. Their blood gets less oxygen.

smoking damages people's health and it can kill

Rice, wheat, fruit, and
vegetables contain many
vital nutrients.

Junk foods with lots
of fat and sugar do not
provide a balanced diet.

Staying Healthy

If you do not use your muscles, they get weak. Your heart is a muscle, too, so the more it is used, the stronger it gets. Exercise makes your heart work harder to send blood to other working muscles.

yoga helps you breathe deeply

A weightlifter has huge muscles but may not be as fit as a runner.

Yoga is a healthy exercise. It teaches people to breathe deeply and brings oxygen into their bloodstreams. Short bursts of exercise are not as good for your heart as longer-lasting exercise, like bicycling or swimming.

Exercise and the right kind of food will keep you fit and healthy all your life.

Glossary

alveoli the tiny pockets of air that make up your lungs.

antibody a substance made by your body that protects your body against illness.

antigens substances in the blood that make it produce antibodies.

artery a main tube that carries fresh blood from your heart to parts of your body.

atrium one of the two small chambers at the top of your heart.

bladder the bag-like part of the body where urine collects.

blood bank a place where blood is stored.

blood vessels the tubes that carry blood around your body.

blood-letting making a patient bleed to help them get well.

capillary one of a network of tiny tubes that carry blood to and from each body part.

carbon dioxide a gas made of carbon and oxygen.

cell a very small part or unit.

chamber an enclosed space. The heart has four chambers.

chemical a substance that can change when joined or mixed with another substance.

clot the joining together of parts of a liquid like blood so that it stops flowing.

deposit something that is put down in layers.

diaphragm a large muscle in your body that separates your chest from your stomach and makes your lungs work.

digestive system the parts of your body used to break down your food into smaller pieces.

donor somebody who gives something to someone else.

energy the power to do work.

fibrin a substance in the blood that helps the blood thicken.

gauge an instrument to measure things.

germ a tiny living thing that can cause disease.

glands parts of the body that make hormones.

heart attack when the heart suddenly stops working properly.

hemophilia an illness that stops the blood from clotting.

hormone a substance made in the body that triggers changes such as growth.

immune when a person cannot catch a disease, because their body has built up the ability to destroy the disease.

kidneys bean-shaped organs in the body that get rid of waste water from the blood.

lungs the two sponge-like parts of the body used for breathing.

lymph a colorless liquid that is made in the body. Lymph helps in cleaning the blood and in fighting disease.

microscope an instrument that makes tiny things look larger.

muscle a type of material in the body that can shorten itself to produce movement.

nutrient the part of any food that can be used by the body for health and growth.

oxygen a gas found in air and water. We cannot breathe without oxygen.

pacemaker an instrument put in the body to make the heart beat steadily.

pituitary gland a part of the body that sends out hormones to control growth.

platelets round-shaped blood cells that stop bleeding.

pressure the action of something pressing on, or against, something.

pulse a single beat of sound or light.

pulse rate the speed at which your heart is working to pump the blood around your body.

ribs a series of long bones that form a cage around parts of the chest.

scab the covering built up in layers over a cut to stop the bleeding and help new skin to grow underneath it.

stethoscope an instrument that a doctor uses to listen to the sounds in your body.

temperature how hot or cold your body is.

thermometer an instrument to measure temperature.

vaccination a dose of specially-treated germs strong enough for the body to learn to protect itself against them.

valve a kind of flap that opens to let a liquid pass in and out of a pipe or tube.

vein a main tube that carries stale blood from all over the body to the heart and lungs.

ventricle one of two chambers in the lower part of the heart.

villi tiny finger-like cells lining the small intestine walls.

windpipe the tube that goes between the throat and the lungs to carry air to the lungs.

x ray a ray that can see through solid objects.

Index

alveoli 19
antibody 22
antigens 32
arteries 10, 15, 16, 36, 42
atrium 12, 13

bladder 25
blood 4, 8–22, 24–26, 28–37, 39, 42, 44, 45
blood bank 35
blood-letting 8
blood pressure 16, 17
blood vessels 10, 14, 27

capillaries 10, 14, 19, 21
carbon dioxide 19, 20
cells 9, 10, 14, 15, 20, 21, 31, 35

chambers 12
chemicals 35
clot 30, 31, 35
cold-blooded animals 26

deposits 36
diaphragm 18
digestive system 24
donor 35

exercise 16, 17, 27, 44, 45

fats 36, 42
fibrin 31
first aid 40

germs 21, 22, 23, 27, 30, 31
glands 23, 28

heart attack 36
heartbeat 4, 5, 9, 10, 16, 29, 38, 39
hemophilia 37
hormones 28, 29

immunity 22

kidneys 14, 25

large intestine 25

leeches 8
lungs 10, 12, 13, 18–20, 42
lymph 23
lymph nodes 23

microscope 9, 15, 20, 31, 39

oxygen 10, 12, 17, 19, 20, 42, 45

pacemaker 39
platelets 21, 30
pulse rate 10, 16

red blood cells 20, 21, 31

scab 21, 31
stethoscope 9

temperature 26, 27
thermometer 27

valves 12, 13, 15
veins 10, 15
ventricle 12, 13

warm-blooded animals 26
white blood cells 21–23

© Heinemann Children's Reference 1990
Artwork © BLA Publishing Limited 1987

Material used in this book first appeared in Macmillan World Library: HOW OUR BODIES WORK: *The Heart and Blood.* Published by Heinemann Children's Reference

Photographic credits
(t = top b = bottom l = left r = right)
cover: © Steven Burr Williams/The Image Bank
4 Science Photo Library; 6 The Hutchinson Library; 7 Vivian Fifield; 8t Royal College of Physicians; 8b Science Photo Library; 9 Ann Roman Picture Library; 10 Science Photo Library; 13 J. Allen Cash; 14 Biophoto Associates; 15 Vision International; 16 S. & R. Greenhill; 17t Science Photo Library; 17b S. & R. Greenhill; 19 J. Allan Cash; 20 Biophoto Associates; 21t, 21b Science Photo Library; 23 S. & R. Greenhill; 26 Frank Lane Picture Agency; 26t Vision International; 27b S. & R. Greenhill; 29t Vision International; 29b LAT Photographic; 31 Science Photo Library; 32l, 32r Biophoto Associates; 33t J. Allan Cash; 33b, 34, 35t, 35b Science Photo Library; 36 St. Bartholomew's Hospital; 37 Dr. T. Korn/Ysbyty Gwynedd; 38, 39t, 39b Science Photo Library; 42 S. & R. Greenhill; 44t ZEFA; 44b Vision International; 45 S. & R. Greenhill